The BAHAMAS

A Colorful and Concise History

To
Joanne, Vivian, Joyce, Lori & Lynn

Copyright 1992 JSA Publications, Inc.

All rights reserved. No part of this book may be used or reproduced in any manner without the consent of the publisher. For additional information, questions or comments, please write the publisher:

Scrivener Press
P.O. BOX 37175
Oak Park, MI 48237

First Edition 1992
ISBN: 0-929957-01-6
Library of Congress Catalog Number 91-62785
Printed in the United States of America
2 3 4 5 6 7 8 9 0

Additional copies of this and our other books maybe ordered by calling 1-800-345-0096

Bahamas   ISBN   0-929957-01-6

The
BAHAMAS
A Colorful and Concise History

by

Joe Ajlouny

Scrivener Press

Acknowledgements

Thanks are due to the following for their help, support and encouragement:

June I. Parker, Lisa A. McDonald, Terri Rogers, Paul Ammar, Susan Graham, Marilyn Krol, Christian Klaver, Janet Puttick, and my family and friends. Each of them owns a part of my heart and I am grateful for all their assistance.

In the Bahamas, I wish to thank the cordial staffs of the Nassau Public Library, the Bahamas Historical Society, the Bahamas Tour Office for their patience and guidence during my research. I asked a lot of questions and marveled at their ability to answer them.

Thanks also to Gregory Lee of the Bahamian News for his gracious support, and to Ray Harrison of the Bahamas Ministry of Tourism for his helpful suggestions.

Original illustrations by June I. Parker and Joanne Nicola. Maps courtesy of U.S. State Department Office of Public Affairs.

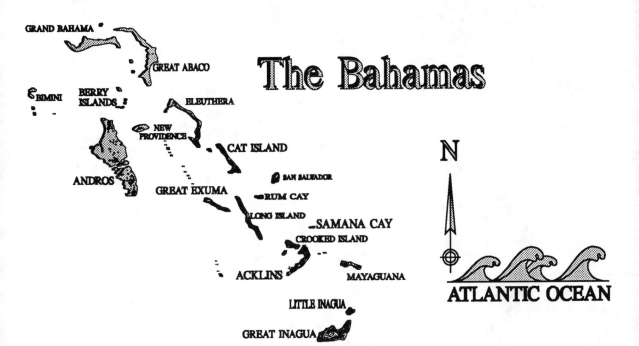

INTRODUCTION

*" There are fish here so unlike ours, that it is a marvel. No man would not wonder at them or be anything but delighted to see them."**

The sprawling Bahama islands rest in the turquoise western waters of the mid-Atlantic Ocean. They begin only 50 miles from the Florida coast and stretch in a southeasterly arc through the Tropic of Cancer to the north Caribbean Sea. The capital city, Nassau, is closer to Los Angeles than is Honolulu. Having more than 700 islands (only about twenty-five are regularly inhabited), the Bahamas spread out over 100,000 square miles of ocean. With a total combined land mass of only 5358 square miles, The Bahamas is one of the smallest nations in the world. Despite its size, it is widely known as a tropical island paradise. Her beauty, expressed in the trees and flowers, the birds and fish and the smiles of her people, is not easily forgotten. These qualities, among countless others, make the Bahamas a favorite vacation destination for millions of Americans,

*An excerpt from the log of Christopher Columbus upon his landing in the Bahamas in 1492

Canadians, Europeans and Latin Americans. It's no wonder why.

The warm gulf stream waters and cool ocean breezes ensure nearly perfect year-round weather. Her proximity to the United States and historical connection to England provides a familiar and inviting environment for all who visit her varied shores. Today, it is not uncommon to find people who visit just for the weekend, long enough for some sun, casino nightlife and a taste of conch (pronounced "Konk") soup, an island specialty. One cannot, of course, escape without hearing the rhythmic pulse of traditional Bahamian music and dance. It reverberates throughout the islands, especially on festive holidays.

In the 1990's, the number of tourists expected to visit the Bahamas will exceed four million per year. Once there, they can enjoy hundreds of activities and sites from Nassau and Freeport, the most metropolitan ports of entry, to Hope Town and Pirates' Well, just two of the hundreds of small, sleepy towns on the "out islands".

The Bahamas have a history too. It is presumed that you'll see and do just about everything you want while you're visiting the islands. I am sure you will become curious about their past. Mark Twain once wrote: "Travel is fatal to prejudice and history, but the cradle of enlightenment." I would hope that this short history, sprinkled as it is with lore and legend of the people and places, serves that noble purpose. Today, the Bahamas are home to about 1.5 million people, 85 percent of whom are Black or mixed. Another 100,000 are seasonal residents, mostly retirees from Britain. Their present differences and their similarities mirror a story of incredible ups and troublesome downs, wonderful successes and tragic failures.

Long before the resorts and arcades were imagined, a clever sailor named Columbus unexpectedly ventured onto her clear and shallow shores. There he found the Lucayan Indians, survivors of an ancient race who lived in simple, peaceful seaside villages. As you will soon learn, the Lucayans would have gladly foregone the historical distinction of welcoming the first Europeans to the New World.

Then, after more than 100 years had passed, adventurous Protestant dissenters landed on the islands and unwittingly surrendered their dominion to the British in exchange for sorely needed aid and goods. The succeeding centuries witnessed many changes of authority and battles between conflicting interests. Like any nation's history, that of the Bahamas is filled with interesting facts and stories unique to its own heritage. Through it all, the Bahamas, land of butterflies and flamingos, stands today as a prosperous and stable democracy in a region where just the opposite has all too often been the case. Therefore, as you enjoy your vacation pay careful attention to historical landmarks and cultural traditions that make the Bahamas unique. See if you can't follow the thread of developments from Columbus' time until today. I promise you will be the wealthier traveler if you do.

CONTENTS

CONTENTS

s is always the case in the study of history, there never is a good place to start. Time is a relentless and unforging rival of mankind, yet is singularly responsible for all the progress that mankind has made on earth. And considering where we were, to where we are today, that passage has rarely been easy or pleasant. Irrespective of your views on the origins of man, the story of mankind is actually not that old. Relative to the age of the universe, or our own planet, we're still in Chapter One. If we skip the prologue and flip past the first several pages, we conveniently arrive at the year 1400 A.D.

Europe and most of the known world was recovering from the Black Plague, that huge and terrible disease that reduced the population by about 40 percent in less than one hundred years. The great European powers of the time, England, France, Spain, Portugal and Holland were engaged in a spirited, but never ending competition for wealth and conquest. But little was known about the world beyond their shores. Maps of the day still showed Jerusalem as the center of the flat earth. The influence of the Catholic Church in all spheres of life was enormous. It was in realization of this influence and a desire to convert it into national prestige that led the great powers of the day to seek goods and riches from beyond the confines of the Mediterranean Sea. The rivalries that continually pitted one or another against each other, or against the great city-states of Italy, however, proved to be less than noble and often unproductive. The travels of Venetian explorer Marco Polo to the east, through Arabia and Asia, to Cathay (China) inspired the glory seekers of the age to explore the earth's surface.

First among their considerations was the

A scroll depicting brothers Marco and Niccolo Polo with their caravan.

promise of riches from the Orient as displayed by Kubla Kahn, ruler of the Mongolian tribesmen, and his ostentatious courtiers. Next came the European desire for exotic eastern goods, such as tea and spices, porcelain and, yes, gunpowder. Polo's journeys, while admirable, were not practical because they were by foot. It took Polo and his entourage five years of difficult caravaning to reach China in the year 1275. Trade by caravan was simply not good enough to satisfy the hungry appetites of European Lords and commercial barons. Moreover, with the rise of the empire of the Ottoman Turks, the land routes to the Far East were cut off. Not being content to rely on the Turks or the Italians for oriental goods, the powers of European commerce, merchants and explorers decided to circumvent the middleman and buy direct.

Sea-going travel and trade exploded with activity in the 15th century. Sea routes were established to Constantinople, the Crimea, Syrma, the India Coast, North Africa and elsewhere. Understandably, there existed great anxiety about the unknown world. This anxiety gradually expressed itself in the form of wanderlust. The century of discovery had arrived. There was a growing debate among sailors, scientists and cartographers concerning the size and shape of the earth. The differences that followed gave rise to a full-fledged war of competition between the European kingdoms for economic conquest and territorial colonization.

Experienced sea captains were very much in

demand. One such man was a Genoese born sailor named Christopher Columbus. Columbus had joined a galley crew at age 14 and survived a sea battle that brought him alone on a floating wooden plank to Portugal.* There he married, worked for his brother-in-law as a merchant and began studying various shipping routes. Columbus was brilliant and a daring and imaginative planner. He was heavily influenced by Florentine astronomer Toscanelli, who encouraged him to design a passage to India by sailing westward. Columbus did so and consequently changed the world.

---

*By the end of the 15th century, Portugal was the undisputed leader in maritime explorations. Bartholomew Diaz and later Vasco de Gama were responsible for opening the eastward passage around Africa's Cape of Good Hope to reach India and subsequently China.

The eager Columbus applied for sponsorship of the expedition to John II of Portugal and Henry VII of England. They both rejected the proposal as too risky. Next he applied to the newly United Kingdom of Spain, which in that day was Portugal and England's constant enemy. Isabela, Queen of Castille' (John II's daughter) who in 1469 married King Ferdinand V of Aragon, was not discouraged by the seeming implausibility of the expedition. She took Columbus on and referred his plans to a panel of advisors. After almost eight long years of on-again off-again discussions, Columbus finally received his charge in January, 1492.

On Friday, August 3, 1492, Columbus set sail aboard the carrrack Santa Maria with 50 men, attended by two smaller caravels, the

Pinta and the Nina, with crews of about 30 men each. After a brief stop in the Canary Islands, they set out on what has become the single most important voyage in history.

Columbus' diary describes the difficulties he encountered with the ocean, navigation--and most importantly--his impatient crew. They had been out to sea longer than any known voyagers to that time. His men were understandably frightened and restless. It must be remembered that at that time the Church had encouraged the belief that only monsters and beasts could inhabit lands not under its spiritual control. Then, in the second week of October, branches were spotted in the water, which was turning from deep blue to turquoise-green. On October 12th, one Rodridgo de Triana, a look-out on the Pinta's forecastle shouted excitingly, *"Tierra, Tierra!"* It was land at last. It being too dangerous to proceed with darkness nearing, Columbus ordered the sails taken down for fear of grounding or encountering reefs. That night, nobody slept. One can only guess what went through the minds of the tired and seasick crewmen. Anticipation ruled. "Are we finally in India, or near it? If not, where are we?"

What the voyagers didn't know was that they had landed on the island of *Guanahani,* a small, low rock formation that stood on the outside edge of the North American continental plate. The island was about twelve miles long and eight miles wide. It was sparsely occupied by a tribe of Arawak Indians, who called themselves Lucayans. The peaceful Lucayans had

come to this and countless other surrounding isles in flight from the cannibalistic Carib Indians. They migrated northward from present day Venezuela and Guyana, upwards through the Lesser Antilles islands of the Caribbean Sea.

Their fear upon seeing the Spanish ships off their shores can hardly be imagined. Initially, they retreated into the woods. They saw three scouting parties disembark and paddle towards them. The superstitious Lucay may have thought that the voyagers had come from heaven and were mythical gods to help them return to their native lands in South America. By the use of sign language, they were able to communicate with each other after only a short time. Columbus noted that his first encounter with the natives was a happy one. He presented them with gifts and quickly won their admiration. By that same afternoon, the bay was filled with the canoes of the natives who were eager to see the ships, the sailors and everything "new" the explorers had to offer them.

Columbus wrote that the Lucayans were a simple and humble people, who offered their help and hospitality in exchange for European goods such as flour, iron nails, shovels and glass. They were simple, seaside village people. Artifacts reveal that they were expert woodcarvers and craftsmen. Little evidence of farming has been uncovered. Accounts by Spanish seamen report that they were deep brown skinned and had flat heads because as infants they were strapped to flat boards. Women wore colorful jewelry, straw skirts and braided their long dark hair. At maturity, men had one ear chopped off. The Lucayans never developed a written form of language; rather their history was related in the oral "story telling" tradition which is unfortunately lost forever.

The gold they wore for ornamentation (they wore little else) particularly interested Colum-

A native Lucayan scene as portrayed by an artist aboard a subsequent armada. Note the clothing of the couple at the left, which shows the early influence of the Europeans.

bus and his crew. The natives described a land called Cubla (Cuba). Columbus thought that they must be referring to Kublai, as in the Khan of China. After only two days, the anxious Columbus, and his crew set out once again in search of riches. Unbeknownst to the Lucayans, however, he first planted the Spanish flag and renamed the island, San Salvador, in honor of the Christian Savior.

For the following 20 days, Columbus hopped from one island to another, renaming them all after first claiming them under Spain's dominion. He brought about a half dozen Lucayans with him to help him navigate the shallow, treacherous waters of the region. Columbus called the area baja mar meaning "shallow sea". It is from this observation, also noted in his diary, that the islands came to be called the Bahamas.

At the beginning of December, 1492, Columbus left the Bahamas, never to return. His mission, however, was to impact upon the Lucayans greatly. He went on to discover Cuba and Hispaniola* (Little Spain), Puerto Rico and in three subsequent voyages, the majority of the islands in the vast blue Caribbean Sea. On Hispaniola, where the native Tainos Indians were likewise simple, kind, and trusting, Columbus discovered gold. Though it was obvious that he had blundered in his view of the size and shape of the earth, it is fair to say that it was a splendid blunder. Never before had so vast an area been discovered without a clue of its

*The island of present day Haiti and the Dominican

existence.

Over the next 40 years, Spain, ecstatic about its findings in the New World, invested heavily in the mining of gold and silver there. The Lucayan people of the Bahamas, and other native island Indians were captured and enslaved to enrich their conquerors. The Spaniards considered them heathens and so did not hesitate to treat them with incalculable cruelty and neglect. Columbus, in his diary, had correctly surmised that the Lucayans would be an easy people to subjugate. He thought of them as "bashful, quiet and obedient." He wrote to Queen Isabela that the Lucayans and other island natives would make ideal servants.

It is sad to say, especially since Columbus and those who followed him ostensibly came to enlighten the natives to Christianity, that the introduction of "the white man" effectively ended an entire civilization. Not only were the Lucayans wiped out, but so were the Caribs, the Tainos, and all the other native Arawak tribes of the region. The Spanish conquerors failed to see in them the faintest hope of humanity. Thus, despite Queen Isabela's orders to protect the natives, they were "used" as labor and were so badly mistreated that it was not uncommon for them to be slaughtered en masse for the slightest transgressions. Others died of European imported diseases, such as smallpox, typhus and gonorrhea. Still others fled into the hills or committed suicide rather than become slaves.

By 1525, the Bahama islands were completely vacant. The Lucayans as a people were destroyed. With the perished of the island inhabitants, the Bahamas languished without note. The Spanish, believing them to be useless, never settled the islands. They were instead used as storage facilities and shipmending stations. The Spaniards established their first major settlement at Santa Domingo on Hispaniola. Then, in rapid succession they conquered and colonized Cuba, Puerto Rico, Mexico and Central America. It would be the British who rediscovered the Bahamas over 100 years later before any more history was made on the islands.

CHAPTER 2   THE ADVENTURERS ARRIVE

A s exploration of the New World continued, the Bahamas were essentially ig-
nored. Compared to the North American and South American mainlands and Central
America to the west, the Bahama islands offered no clear prospects. It must be remembered that the Old World was in a period of
commercial expansion, what we would call
today "a commercial revolution." This neces-
sarily directed the resources of the discovering
nations toward clearly exploitable territories.

The Bahamas, being small, scattered, flat and
dry, simply did not compare to the rich poten-
tial lands of other larger lands.

The European powers, jealous of the Arab
and Italian dominance of Asian trade, were
anxious for new markets. In 50 short years,
Spain conquered Mexico, Columbia, Venezuela and was reaching as far south as modern
day Chile and Argentina. Portugal colonized
Brazil and delved deep into its interior in search
of mineral wealth. The age of the conquering

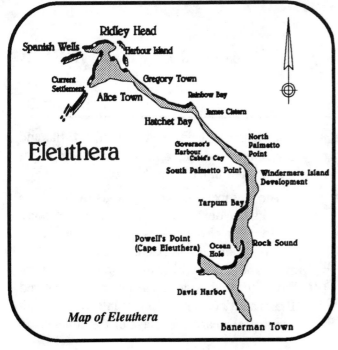

Map of Eleuthera

Armada had reached its glory.

By 1625 the English had already established the first settlement at Jamestown, Massachusetts and had claimed the islands of Barbados, St. Kitts and Nevis in the Caribbean Sea. In the excitement that followed, new frontiers in the west were claimed by France, Spain, Portugal, Holland, Denmark and even Austria. The monarchies of these countries freely granted proprietary interests to loyal noblemen in the hope that they would develop the new lands and thereby create new riches for their kingdoms. The Church encouraged these efforts in the hope of adding new and loyal parishioner- and wealth to its coffers. Jesuit mission-

sent out with the conqueror did their best to curb the abuses of the labor system but found themselves helpless in the face of greed and the thirst for power.

In 1629 England's King Charles I deeded the lands of Carolina, so named in his honor, to his ally Sir Robert Heath. The formal documents included this additional phrase "... and also those our islands of Bahama." Unfortunately, the times in England were not pleasant. Charles was locked in a bitter fight with rivals who sought his ouster. Civil and religious persecution steadily rose and gripped the entire British kingdom. Those religious dissenters who objected to the strong influence of the Anglican Church, on the one hand and the English throne on the other, called themselves Puritans. Finally, in 1646, pro-Parliament forces led by Oliver Cromwell, a Puritan himself, captured London. King Charles I was hanged and Heath died in exile. Due to the calamity, no attempt was made to settle or explore the Bahamas.*

As religious intolerance and social discord grew, many thousands set out for the New World and became the pilgrims of a new age. Many were driven into exile but most sought it freely. Some went to the North American

* Cromwell did launch a fleet to the Caribbean in 1654, it landed first at Barbados where recruits were enlisted. Then, after a decisive defeat by Spain in Hispaniola, the expedition went on to defeat Spain in Jamaica. The Bahamas were bypassed by the entire expedition.

the colonies that proclaimed their independence in 1776. Others had fled to Bermuda, the lonely island in the mid-North Atlantic that served as a port for all English sea-going traffic. Since 1612, when it was first settled, dissenters had flocked there in great numbers. But the turmoil from home reached Bermuda as well. A small group of Puritans and clergy, angry with the growing official British dominance of the island, decided to flee again, this time to the south, to the islands of Bahama.

In 1648 Captain William Sayle, the jilted Governor of Bermuda, established an expedition called The Company of Adventures for the Plantations of the Islands of Eleutheria*.

---

*Eleutheria, later shortened to Eleuthera, was named for the mythical land of freedom in ancient

With a group of about 60 on board three small ships, the voyagers set out triumphantly and with hope. They drew up a charter called "Articles and Orders," which was in effect the first constitution of the Bahamas. It was also the first of its kind anywhere, guaranteeing as it did, absolute personal freedoms.

The voyage was not easy. The heavy waters of the Atlantic tossed the ships, a frigate and two trawlers, and finally smashed them against the reef of the island of *Cigatou*, as Eleuthera was then called. (The treacherous reef has since been known as the "Devil's Backbone".) Two of the three ships were destroyed and all of their provisions were lost in the darkness. Despite the fact that many lost their lives as a result, the adventurers managed to survive.

They made their way to a large cave at the north end of the island and settled there and on the neighboring small islands, which they called Cays (pronounced "key" as in Key West). It is safe to say that the adventurers probably regretted their decision to leave Bermuda. There was, however, no way of returning.

Their new island home, known today as Preacher's Cave, was hardly what they hoped to find. It was hot and dry and food was unavailable, except fish and wild fruit. They struggled for several years and eaked out a minimal existence. Sayle and a handful of others patched up one craft and set sail in search of assistance. Slowly aid did arrive, first from Bermuda and then from the territory of Carolina, which was linked to the Bahamas by the original proprietary deed. The island was renamed Eleutheria and the towns of Spanish Wells and Dunmore Town were founded and settled. Within ten years a new port was established on the central island of New Providence.

In time, commercial contacts from Bermuda enroute to America, reached New Providence Island and the natural harbor at Nassau soon spawned a booming town. Contacts also emerged between the two main island colonies of New Providence and Eleutheria. In response to financial concerns and lawlessness, they applied to the British Governor of Carolina for assistance. Lord Anthony Ashley Cooper, 1st Earl of Shaftsbury and a powerful English aristocrat, succeeded in responding to their requests. Slowly cotton, tobacco, and vegetable

quests. Slowly cotton, tobacco, and vegetable farming were developed, but always under difficult circumstances due to the dry and shallow nature of the Bahamian soil. Stark conditions for the colonists improved gradually. The overpopulation of Bermuda and the incentives provided by the proprietors encouraged more people to settle in the Bahamas.* New settlements were started all over the two islands, and then on Abaco, Exuma and elsewhere.

Yet for all the good intentions and hard efforts, life remained a struggle on the islands. Experience taught the British that the Bahamas weren't worth the effort and expense of exploit-

*In 1656, Bermuda exiled hundreds of troublesome residents. Most fled to the Bahamas. Many slaves were promised freedom on Eleuthera and once there, they got it.

Eluthera's Coat of arms depicting the Bible, settlement tools, the British flag and a pineapple.

ing, certainly not in comparison to the vastness of her North and South American continental mainlands. The colonists that remained managed the best they could, though times were always hard. The English frequently shipped slaves to the islands in an effort to populate the farms and plantations. Several large plantations were developed as a result, yielding cotton, sugar, citrus fruit, tobacco and other crops. Numerous fishing settlements also sprang up and trade with passing ships, though usually illegal, helped maintain the poor villagers and brought them goods and news of the outside world.

In succeeding years, English animosity with Spain imposed upon the islanders a political role. When England claimed rights in sunken vessels in Bahamian waters, Spain reacted strongly, attacking English settlements throughout the islands. In 1684, the Spanish plundered the initial Eleutheria settlement at Preacher's Cave. Though Spain could have conquered the Bahamas anytime it wanted, for some unknown reason never did. This would prove to be a mistake, as we shall learn.

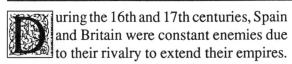uring the 16th and 17th centuries, Spain and Britain were constant enemies due to their rivalry to extend their empires. Not unlike the tendency today, colonialists were quick to employ mercenary manpower to foil the exploits of the other. Privateers, armed vessels of independent sailors for hire, were regularly commissioned both in and out of wartime to prey upon colonial ships and their cargos. The motivation of the privateers was not difficult to understand. The poverty and despair that sailors and settlers found themselves in naturally caused them to look for other means of survival.* Accordingly, cargo salvaging and treasure trove hunting became the best hope for those that remained on the poor islands and surrounding cays of the Bahamas.

The Spanish vessels had no alternative but to navigate the dangerously shallow and reef

---

* The practice of Privateering, being dangerous and unreliable, was outlawed by the Declaration of Paris Treaty in 1856. The U.S. did not sign it until after the American Civil War (1861-65).

filled waters of the region in order to deliver their booty home. They lost so many ships that fierce competition arose for the salvage of cargo, supplies and gold. Encouraged by the British Navy, many islanders, joined by fortune hunters from various lands, became pirates, wreckers and buccaneers. The situation was further magnified when the main pirate enclave of Port Royal in Jamaica was destroyed by a tidal wave in 1692. It is estimated that more than 500 fierce and experienced pirates resettled in and around the small islands of the Bahamas. The toll that they took on Spanish main shipping so infuriated the Spanish Governor of Havana that in 1703 he sent troops to destroy the main settlement at Nassau. Over the period of the following 15 years, Nassau was attacked by both Spaniards and the French over two dozen times. These events caused a series of weak Bahamian governors to collaborate with the pirates and buccaneers to defend the islands. Then, in exchange for a relaxation of the laws against them, the criminal seamen often shared their booty with the fledgling government and its supporters. The few remaining honest settlers fled for safer places, not being welcome or safe in the midst of the Spaniards who soon controlled the port and town.

Thus, during the period through the dawn of the 1700's, Nassau became a lawless city, occupied by an untamed group of criminals and outlaws without government or allegiance. The marauding seamen attacked any and all shipping. There are stories of how they lured unwitting ships into dangerous rocks and reefs in order to burglarize their contents or hijack them outright. For the pirates, Nassau was ideal. It lay astride the major trade routes between the Caribbean, America and Europe. Its strategic harbor with the barrier of Paradise Island, was excellent for escaping from the warships that guarded merchant vessels.

So began the swashbuckling and treacherous deeds of the pirates that have remained so strong in the folklore of the region. There were as many as two thousand pirates operating in various gangs on all parts of New Providence. History and legend have not forgotten their names. There was Edward "Blackbeard" Teach, Charles Vane, Peter Hynd, Benjamin "Cutter" Horngold and "Calico" Jack Rackman and his infamous buxom sidekicks, Anne Bonney and Mary Read. Perhaps the most successful of them all, Henry Morgan, grew so wealthy as a result that he became respectable enough to be named the English Governor of Jamaica.

In response to the complaints from interested parties in the region, London terminated the proprietary lease and made the Bahamas a Crown Colony. She dispatched a seasoned naval captain and national hero named Captain Woode Rogers to restore order. He and his crew of four warships arrived in Nassau in July 1718. As the new Governor-General, he seized control of New Providence and offered amnesty to all pirates and buccaneers if they would stop their larcenous ways. A surprising number took up his pledge and returned to pursue more mundane endeavors. Rather than fight, and risk disaster, Rogers wisely offered safe passage out of the islands to all remaining Spaniards, who incidentally had taken control of all the large homes and plantations they could find. Rogers found Nassau to be a filthy, squalid place. He lived onboard his ship rather than occupy the old battered governor's estate in the center of town. He and his crew quickly reclaimed and improved Fort Nassau and Fort

Edward Teach

(1666? - 1718)

Better known as "Blackbeard" Teach (sometimes known as Thatch) was a British privateer before becoming a dangerous pirate in both Caribbean and Atlantic waters. He was killed in battle by ships sent by the governor of Virginia, whose colony suffered significant losses at the hands of Teach and his henchmen.

Montagu and enlisted regular garrisons to be permanently stationed there. Next he ordered every able-bodied person to clean the streets and wells in an effort to rid the towns of rats and disease. Next, he encouraged settlers from neighboring islands such as Jamaica, Bermuda, Tortuga and Barbados to settle on New Providence and Abaco by offering free land and protection from attacks.

A persuasive personality enabled Captain Rogers to obtain modest funding from the Crown permitting him to rebuild the city and clear the harbor. He also started new plantations including one for himself on the scale of those elsewhere in Britain's bustling empire. In an effort to bolster the population of the islands, he issued a proclamation guaranteeing freedom for slaves from Bermuda and the American colonies. Many thousands responded over the years and henceforth, blacks would be the majority race on the islands. Rogers also restructured the island government, unified the legislature and appointed an executive counsel to advise him on matters relating to social development.

In 1721, Rogers was recalled to England to answer for his debts. Not only had he spent all of his own money in furthering his efforts but he also unwisely guaranteed the debts of others. Like other plantation owners in the Bahamas, he found the going rough. The farms they had established frequently failed. Without a stable industry, most islanders found life to be harsh and unfulfilling. Many fortunes were gained

and lost in the Bahamas, and those that lost usually left never to return. Still others returned to pirating. It was during this period that many settlers, in search of greener pastures, traveled to and settled down on islands of the Bahamas such as Abaco, Exuma, San Salvador, Bimini, Cat Island and Long Island. Rogers spent eight years in debtors prison before being released on condition that he return to the Bahamas. Apparently the British could

---

Henry Morgan

(1635-1688)

A kidnap victim in his youth, Morgan was taken to Barbados where he learned to sail and navigate. He was the most successful pirate of the age, and successfully eluded Spain's numerous attempts to apprehend him

---

find nobody else to volunteer for the post. Rogers returned to Nassau in 1729 and died there three years later. An imposing commemorative statue was erected in central Nassau on the centennial of his death.

Close ties inevitably developed between the Bahamian settlers and the colonists of North America. The majority of the islands' agricultural output was now being exported to the

Woodes Rogers

(1671 - 1732)

Though he was the top British official on The Bahamas, Rogers was initially hired to command a privateering expedition to steal back riches lost by the crown. He is credited with successfully resisting Spain's efforts to reclaim the islands. His successors were less fortunate.

Carolinas and Virginia. Disappointed settlers frequently moved to the American colonies rather than return to England. In some instances, colonists moved to the islands to escape the heavy taxes and regulations that England imposed on America but not on the Bahamas. Runaway slaves regularly surrendered themselves to Bahamian merchants or were stowaways on their ships. Naturally, the Bahamas policy of offering freedom to escaped slaves from America irked colonial governors there.

In some cases, repatriation was forced on the islands by way of economic blackmail. The weak and vulnerable position of the islands was at once evident. In fact, the beleaguered islands would not receive a reprieve until their American cousins decided to kick the British out. As important as that event was for the future of the colonies, it was equally important for the islands. The destiny of the two countries would thereafter be tied together.

CHAPTER 4

A LOYALISTS' RETREAT

nrest at home, as well as controversy with both France and Spain, ensured the eventual dissolution of British power in the New World. When the American Revolutionary War broke out, hundreds of loyalists fled to the Bahamas for safety. Many brought their fortunes, their families and slaves with them. Most escaped to Eleuthera, while others settled wherever their boats by chance took them.

Hurting because of the British blockade of major American ports, the rebellious colonists sent a group of small ships to Nassau, in 1777 to raid for arms and ammunition. Led by Commodore Ezekial Hopkins, they captured a huge supply of gunpowder without having to do battle. The U.S. attack in Nassau was probably the most successful military mission ever performed by the U.S. military. For a period of three days, the American rebel flag was raised over Fort Nassau. No shots were fired; they got what they wanted and even returned with the

British Governor General of the islands as hostage.

As the war of independence progressed, retreating British forces and loyalists moved into Florida, a Spanish territory. The angry Spanish responded by once again invading and occupying Nassau. The British fought back. They recruited pirate types to disrupt shipping between the American rebels and their French and Spanish allies. The campaign was successful but it could not affect the final outcome. When a peace treaty was finally signed and the colonies achieved their independence, Florida was ceded to Spain, and the British were awarded the Bahamas as a consolation prize. As we have already seen, neither the U.S. nor Spain had much interest in the islands. The prevailing attitude of both governments seems to have been, "You wanted them, you got them." Thus, as a result of the Treaty of Versailles, which was signed by all the parties on Sept. 3, 1783, the remaining British were expelled from Florida. Accordingly, most set out for the Bahamas, the nearest British colony.

The exploits of a loyalist, Colonel Andrew Deveaux, and his followers, have gone down in history as one of the more cunning upsets in conflict studies. Deveaux was an embattled leader of a mismatched group of South Carolina loyalists who had fled to eastern Florida to escape persecution by the bitter colonists. When he learned the territory was to remain Spain's, he and his followers purchased several ships with gold they brought with them and they sailed off to Eleuthera in the spring of 1783.

Once there, they made plans to recapture Nassau, as it was still being occupied by Spanish troops. With a rag-tag crew of about 200 men, nearly all the able-bodied white men on the islands, Deveaux, by a series of inventive maneuvers, tricked the Spanish into withdrawing. The Union Jack once again waved over Nassau.* With the restoration of British control of the Bahamas, fleeing loyalists flocked to

*There has been a great deal of speculation whether the Spaniards, who were after all very experienced soldiers, actually fell for Deveaux's tactics or whether they withdrew under orders pursuant to the peace treaty. It is not known whether word of the treaty had gotten to the Spaniards by November 9, 1785 the day they finally evacuated the forts of Nassau Harbor.

Andrew Deveaux

(1746-1798)

Not wishing to rule following his triumph, the Colonel retired to a large plantation on Cat Island.

the islands. Between the years 1784 to 1789, the population increased four times to almost 12,000. They came from Virginia, the Carolinas, Florida and even from as far as New York and New Jersey in the north. Of that number, three-fourths were Negro slaves or freed slaves who accompanied their masters.

Many of the British immigrants were former officers and colonial government officials. They reconstituted the Bahamas House of Assembly, enacted a code of laws and established the first real central Bahamian government. New buildings were constructed, as were a water tower and several churches, schools and hospitals. John Wells, a loyalist printer from Maryland, established The Gazette, Nassau's first newspaper in 1785.

To encourage agricultural development, the head of every family in the colony was granted at least 40 acres of land, plus 20 additional acres for each family member and each slave. Farming of cotton, tobacco, pineapple, figs, grapes, tomatoes and sugar began once again. Sheep and cattle were brought in from Bermuda and livestock farming was introduced for the first time. Under the stewardship of Sir William Murray, former Governor of Virginia and newly appointed Governor of the Bahamas, the islands' defenses were fortified. Fort Nassau and Fort Montague, aging and battered remnants from Rogers' day, were refurbished; massive Fort Charlotte, a feat of architectural ingenuity, was built and manned on Nassau's highest hill. Murray was knighted with the title Lord Dunmore. Dunmore Town on Harbor

Island in Eleuthera was named in his honor.

Exports rose steadily for the first time and regular commercial traffic was scheduled into Nassau Harbor. Alas, things went poorly. A number of large plantations, having been struck by insects and worms, failed utterly. The Bahamas, while rich in some resources, totally lacked many essential others. The cost of importing so much from abroad made it impossible for the farmers to compete with their products. One by one, they went bust and left for England, not unlike their countrymen 100 years earlier.

When the War of 1812 broke out, the Bahamas were hardly in a position to aid the British, except as a port for suppliers and as a place of refuge. In 1813, aided by the French, a horde of U.S. privateers sacked and burned Spanish Wells in retaliation for the British blockade of U.S.-bound shipping. The British Navy subsequently ordered a system of lighthouses built to protect the islands and direct their vessels toward the appropriate islands. Many of the light houses still stand today. Some are still used for commercial purposes, while others only decorate the Bahamian landscape.

With the flight of the majority of the white settlers, the population and wealth of the islands sank measurably. Left behind were poor and under educated slaves, dilapidated farms and aimless, broken farmers who could not afford to do anything other than pray for relief. What little commercial activity remained was all but blotted out with the abolishment of the slave trade in 1807.

When slavery itself was finally abolished in the British colonies in 1834, those few plantations that were able to survive finally collapsed. As Europeans fled, more blacks arrived, fleeing from the American south where slavery was at its height of cruelty. In addition, some West Indies slave traders "dumped" their captives on nearby islands to avoid the expense of returning them to eastern Africa. At once poverty and deprivation spread like a cancer. With no capital or support, life for the freed men and their families was harsh and unhopeful.

By 1850, the population of all the islands

A typical slave auction poster. By 1829, slaves were in great demand due to protestations from abolishionists in the U.S. and Canada.

TO BE SOLD & LET
BY PUBLIC AUCTION,
On MONDAY the 18th of MAY. 1829,
UNDER THE TREES.

FOR SALE,
THE THREE FOLLOWING
SLAVES,
viz.

HANNIBAL, about 30 Years old, an excellent House Servant, of Good Character.
WILLIAM, about 35 Years old, a Labourer.
NANCY, an excellent House Servant and Nurse.
The MEN belonging to "LEECH'S" Estate, and the WOMAN to Mrs D. SMIT

TO BE LET,
On the usual conditions of the Hirer finding them in Food, Clo'in-, and Medical ance,
THE FOLLOWING
MALE and FEMALE
SLAVES,
OF GOOD CHARACTERS.

ROBERT BAGLEY, about 20 Years old, a good House Servant.
WILLIAM BAGLEY, about 18 Years old, a Labourer.
JOHN ARMS, about 18 Years old.
JACK ANTONIA, about 40 Years old, a Labourer.
PHILIP, an Excellent Fisherman.
HARRY, about 27 Years old, a good House Servant.
LUCY, a Young Woman of good Character, used to House Work and the Nursery.
ELIZA, an Excellent Washerwoman.
CLARA, an Excellent Washerwoman.
FANNY, about 14 Years old, House Servant.
SARAH, about 14 Years old, House Servant.

Also for Sale, at Eleven o'Clock,
Fine Rice, Gram, Paddy, Books, Muslins, Needles, Pins, Ribbons, &c. &c.

AT ONE O'CLOCK, THAT CELEBRATED ENGLISH HORSE
BLUCHER,

combined had decreased to about 6,000. Nassau had endured a period of sustained economic depression. The settlers of Eleuthera, the Abacos, Grand Bahama, Bimini, and elsewhere all languished in relative solitude. Farming and fishing, the only livelihoods the islands promised, proved sufficient for the remaining inhabitants to survive, but just barely. Elsewhere, ex-slaves who failed to find work as labor on the remaining plantations, founded lonely fishing villages and slowly developed craft making skills to barter with infrequent visitors. In relative isolation, the islanders developed a genuine culture of their own. Music, dancing, festive celebrations and craft making all came into their own as distinct Bahamian variations. Modest churches of various Christian denominations were built and religion became a very important part of every islander's life.

But as everywhere in the West, the years leading up to the 20th century promised great change. The industrial revolution was in full swing and European monarchies had either collapsed or were driven out of most of the Americas. The Bahamas weathered these changes without actually experiencing them. The world outside, however, managed to peek its head in, and liking what it saw, never chose to leave.

Despite their distance from England, the Bahamas received visitors who regularly spent their winter months in low rent seaside houses and cottages. The warm weather and clean air enticed some; others were attracted by their desire to observe and study the wonderful variety of tropical birds and fish. The mythical Fountain of Youth, touted by Spanish naval captain Juan Ponce de Leon, was said to exist on Bimini. These fountains were really just hot springs which exist today in many places throughout the islands. They proved to be particularly popular and succeeded in luring a good deal of business away from Switzerland and Germany, whose baths were highly praised for their therapeutic mystique.

Visitors from America started arriving regularly when the Cunnard steamship lines commenced monthly voyages to Nassau in 1860. In anticipation, the Royal Victoria Hotel was built and opened in 1861. As grand as it was for its time, it sadly became a victim of circumstance, for the American Civil War broke out the very same year.

The impact the war had on the islands was significant. The Bahamas had always been largely dependent on the importation of supplies from the U.S. Any interruption of the flow of commerce was, therefore, very costly. For example, the U.S. government had ordered a halt to U.S. merchant traffic to Nassau during the Battle of 1812 because of their role in the British war effort. As a result, Bahamian residents suffered great hardships. As it retained its English character, the Bahamas had not yet escaped the prejudice that many Americans still felt against the British government.

When the war between the States erupted, President Lincoln ordered a blockade of all southern ports. The South, as agricultural in nature, was largely dependent on imports for weapons and ammunition. The Bahamas, being the nearest foreign territory, quickly responded to the opportunities the war represented. British and French made supplies and munitions were speedily delivered to the Confederate Army for cash, crops and gold. By April 1863, the blockade had proved impossible for the North to enforce. The British government landed sorely needed cannons and guns in Florida in exchange for tons of cotton and tobacco. Many fortunes were made in the arms trade and the Bahamas, especially Nassau, experienced an immediate boom in activity. When the Confederate government threatened to halt its purchases because stowaway slaves were receiving amnesty on the island, the Bahamian authorities quickly agreed to "smoke out" all ships before they left southern ports. The island treasury benefitted greatly from the imposition of import and export duties too. Bay Street in central Nassau was widened and extended. Gas lamps were erected in the city and many new buildings and houses were constructed. For the first time in its history, the Nassau-based government began to invest in improvements on the outer islands, which in the past had always languished on their own. Thus, small schools and hospitals were found-ed, streets and towns were built and incentives were approved to encourage population growth and agricultural development on the "out" islands.

With prosperity and commercial activity also

The harvesting of sugar cane was the chief indus-try of the Bahamas. Above, a plantation boiling house where sugar was processed. A by-product was molasses, from which rum is distilled.

came crime and disease, so much so that it threatened the very nature of the Bahamas' openness. Strict laws against gambling and public drunkenness were enacted. Whereas 100 years, before the government could not even afford to maintain a militia of a dozen men, by 1864 the Bahamas police force and the first regular courthouse were founded in comparative splendor.

With the victory of the Union cause, the Bahamas economy again collapsed. Confederate currency, upon which much of the wealth was based, was now worthless. Emigration of prominent citizens again took place. The Royal Victoria Hotel, which had served as headquarters for many war profiteers, closed quietly for lack of business. Elsewhere, strug-

Sponge fishing was but one of numerous methods Bahamians employed to cultivate the sea.

gling farmers and fishermen, anxious for the resumption of trade with the U.S., were forced out of business by high import duties placed on their products in retaliation for their wartime deeds. The British Parliament slowly invested more money and incentives to spur new economic activity. For the next 20 years, England would be its biggest trading partner, followed by Jamaica, Bermuda and Cuba respectively.

The planting and harvesting of sisal, a fibrous plant that grows nicely in dry arid soil, lured several English businessmen, among them future British Prime Minister Neville Chamberlain. His wealthy father Joseph Chamberlain owned the Andros Fibre Company and sent young Neville there to operate it. Sisal is an elemental part of twine and rope. Sponge har-vesting was also developed on Eleuthera and several other islands, as was salt panning and pearl harvesting. The younger Chamberlain moved to the Abacos and established a pineapple plantation. His former residence in New Plymouth on Green Turtle Cay is still an island tourist attraction.

Despite these encouraging activities, the island as a whole, suffered from continued economic depression. Though slavery had long been abolished, the conditions under which the majority of the islanders lived were rather piti-ful. Basic necessities such as medicine and clothing were in short supply. Once again, hardship and isolation were all one could expect from life.

Tourism slowly caught on as Americans discovered the romance of foreign travel. The Cunard Lines resumed steamship service in 1866, a journey which took five days from New York. The island government reopened the Royal Victoria Hotel. Florida railroad baron, Henry Flagler, became convinced that the Bahamas would be an ideal playground for wealthy Americans in search of adventure. First he purchased the Royal Victoria, then he built his own, the huge Colonial Hotel, also in Nassau, in 1900. That same year he offered steamship service from Miami too. In the years preceding World War I, the Bahamas became a favorite vacation destination for wealthy Britons and Americans. The quaint colonial charm of Nassau and so many other towns derived from this time. Beautiful homes and gardens were maintained by most of England's nobility.

This fact alone attracted thousands of curious Americans who wished to hob-nob with the dukes and earls and ladies of distinction. The guns of August 1914, however, once again caused a decline of the island's prospects. The world, with few exceptions beyond Miami, once again put the Bahamas on the proverbial back burner.

CHAPTER 6   BOOTLEGGING FOR DOLLARS

The passage of the 18th Amendment to the U.S. Constitution in 1919 benefited the Bahamas tremendously. Prohibition meant an end to production, distilling, bottling or distribution of alcoholic beverages anywhere in the U.S. The Bahamians, the English and many individual Americans rapidly took advantage of the situation and began highly successful bootlegging and rumrunning operations out of Nassau Harbor.

In 1917, importation of scotch whiskey from England amounted to about 35,000 barrels. By 1922, the amount had increased to 1.65 million barrels. Distilleries for rum, rye, corn whiskey and sour mash quickly opened on many islands and churned out their products. Smooth operators and middlemen, content to exploit the situation, made money on both sides of every transaction. Nassau's ports were bustling with mercantile pursuits as never before. Bahamian bootleggers are largely responsible for America's love affair with French and Italian wines, as these were also exported to secret U.S. ports, both on the Gulf and Atlantic coastlines of the mainland.

Naturally, the Bahamian government welcomed the large revenues that accompanied the liquor trade. The money was used to expand and develop the old sea towns, and for the installation of utilities and public water and sewage systems. Roads were built linking places that formerly could only be reached by boat. The arrival of the automobile in 1915, made roads necessary for the first time in the islands long history.

Tourist traffic from the U.S. and Canada gradually increased in the 1920s, owing to the new prosperity on the continent. The rich and famous so enjoyed the colorful and peaceful islands that they returned each winter holiday

Dunmore Town on Harbor Island circa 1879.

The Royal Victoria Hotel was one of several lavish buildings erected by gun-running profits.

season, as did the lookers and adventurers behind them. Among those of prominence who regularly visited were the Vanderbilts, the Mellons, the Astors, the Morgans, and others. Hollywood stars and show business entertainers soon followed. During this period, the Royal Victoria was refurbished and the sprawling Fort Montagu Beach Hotel made its debut. In 1929, Pan American Airlines commenced daily flights from Miami to Nassau in eight passenger Sikorski seaplanes. Suddenly, the islands were just an hour away from the mainland.

Bahamian citizens, for the most part, finally believed their island home was destined for brighter days. The quality of life and standard of living for the average islander markedly improved. The boom brought many new residents to New Providence, Grand Bahama, Eleuthera and other islands. Most came for the work but others came because they had become enchanted with the beauty and hospitable climate the Bahamas so unselfishly offers.

Then came the stock market crash, and with it, the Great Depression. Naturally, the sudden loss of wealth in the U.S. meant disaster for the Bahamas. Tourist traffic dwindled to a trickle. The economy of the islands, quickly declined. Once again, the Bahamas fell victim to circumstances beyond her control.

The interruption of World War II strained the islands' resources to their limit, yet they played a small, but important role in the Allied war effort. Prior to the U.S. entry into the war, military equipment was often transferred to

Nassau harbor for shipment to British forces in Europe and North Africa. Newly built bomber airplanes were first delivered to the Bahamas for eventual distribution to England by Royal Air Force pilots, as well as by American and Bahamian volunteer flyers. Bahamas ship craftsmen were asked to deliver a large quantity of wooden supply transports and pontoon rafts. Though it appears that these craft were never used in the war effort, the dedication the Bahamas on the way for Great Britain has not been forgotten. The Bahamas Volunteer Defense Force was credited by the Red Cross with rescuing 232 British sailors from torpedoed ships during the war.

During the early stages of the war, wealthy refugees from Britain and Europe fled to the islands in an effort to escape the Nazi *blitzkrieg*.

The most noteworthy arrival was that of the former King of England, Edward VIII and his twice divorced American bride Wallis Warfield Simpson. To the world they were the Duke and Duchess of Windsor but to their friends they were Dicky and Wally. In 1920, when he was the Prince of Wales, Edward visited the Bahamas with his cousin Lord Louis Mountbatten on his famous world tour of the Commonwealth. Admiral Mountbatten was so taken by the islands that he subsequently built a vacation home on Harbor Island, which he and his wife Edwina visited regularly until her death in 1960.

The Duke and Duchess, however, did not come to the Bahamas to flee the war; they were ordered there by his brother King George VI upon the pleading of Winston Churchill. The Prime Minister was alerted to a German plot to lure the Duke into the Axis fold. Hitler saw the dejected and facile ex-king as the ideal ruler of England after the planned Nazi victory. In an effort to remove the ex-King and his wife from the danger of kidnapping, Churchill arranged to have him appointed Royal Governor and Commander in Chief of the Bahama Islands. He arrived from Portugal in 1940 amidst a joyous celebration. Whereas many loyal subjects were deeply upset that Edward had chosen Mrs. Simpson over the Crown, he remained personally very popular because of his kind and simple demeanor. After the war, the British uncovered Nazi diplomatic cables confirming their suspicions of the German plot concerning the Duke.

With the end of the war, interest in the Bahamas again surged in popularity. The advent of air conditioned hotel rooms and regularly scheduled air flights ensured the islands had found a basic, bankable industry upon which her citizens could survive: Tourism.

CHAPTER 7

THE QUIET REVOLUTION

One good thing about the war is that it left Nassau with a large airfield which was conveniently converted into a modern airport in the early 1950's. Nassau International Airport, sometimes still referred to as Windsor Field, served as the main gateway for the thousands of visitors that were continually vacationing on the sunny islands. Construction of new facilities essentially eliminated unemployment. The "Family Islands" also shared in the boom, being preferred by those who enjoy quieter holidays or natural excursions.

In 1950, retired British attorney Stafford Sands was appointed as the first Chairman of the Bahamas Development Board, a quasi-governmental agency charged with overseeing the new construction and expansion. The major hotel giants soon built lavish resorts, golf courses, and beaches. The rise in popularity of cruise ships from the U.S. eastern seaboard added substantial numbers of tourists as well. With the completion of the Nassau Deepwater Harbor in 1969, cruise ship activity exploded. Sands, who was knighted for his work in support of the islands, projected tourist arrival to exceed 1,000,000 per year by 1970. That number was exceeded in the mid 1960s, and was tripled in the 1980s.

The establishment of the Grand Bahama Port Authority in the mid 1950s was the government's most ambitious project ever. Led by Abaco Island lumber baron, Wallace Groves, the GBPA exercised the right of eminent domain for thousands of acres of land and shoreline. Freeport, the cosmopolitan city of the Bahamas was built there from scratch. The going however, was not easy. The government was forced into making costly concessions due to the slow progress Groves experienced in luring foreign business interests to Grand Bahama. It was the intent of the GBPA to create the first modern and permanent industrial area

The Bahamas Oil Refinery on Grand Bahama Island. Photograph courtesy of Freeport Port Authority.

on the islands. Many of those who did, invest in the area, lost to the tune of millions and so withdrew. The natural beauty of the area was not easily accessible to tourists. Roads were then built, swamps were drained and 50,000 more acres were conceded to the Authority for establishing parks, plazas and shopping centers. Finally, in 1963, in an effort to save the entire project, the Bahama government permitted the issuance of a limited number of gambling licenses. The economy of Grand Bahama

The Governor General's residence in central Nassau, which was built upon orders of Governor Richard Fitzwilliam in 1733. The home's pink facade and corinthian columns are particularly beatiful by moonlight. The statue is of Christopher Columbus and was financed by American author Washington Irving.

boomed at once.

Splendid hotels and lavish casinos opened within the year. Freeport quickly became the mecca for Caribbean bound beachcombers and revelry seekers.

Encouraged by the success of Freeport, A & P Supermarket magnate Huntington Hartford led the development of Hog Island, that narrow strip of land that straddles the north shore of New Providence Island. In a matter of a few years, Hog Island, renamed Paradise Island, became the number one tourist port of all the islands. A suspension bridge was created to facilitate travel to and from Nassau. To protect its residents (and to placate its detractors) the government decreed that gambling was allowed for tourists only. Today, spanning the short width of the island, stand the French Cloisters and alongside them, handsomely large Casuarinas trees and beautiful Versailles Gardens. The cloisters were built in the 14th century for a French monastery, but were purchased in the 1920's by William Randolf Hearst for his San Simeon mansion. Dismantled and shipped to California, the cloisters remained in storage until Hartford heard about them from his architects. This touch, among countless clever others, makes Paradise Island a wonderful place to visit for vacationers all over the world.

Behind all of the economic development of the islands, stood the cooperative but alienated Black majority. Though under the law they enjoyed equal rights, segregation was as much a practice on the islands as it was in the American south. "White Only", that dreaded sign of racial prejudice, was displayed prominently at island hotels, restaurants and theaters. Civil rights legislation banning segregation was not enacted until 1950.

While some Blacks served in the House of Assembly, none held high office or sat in the prestigious upper house, the Legislative Council. Though Blacks constituted 80 percent of the population in 1950, they held less than one sixth of the assembly seats. As in America, Black consciousness rose quickly after the war. For the first time, a majority of the islands inhabitants came to resent the overriding control of their government by the British Parliament in London.

In 1953, several young and educated Black leaders founded the Progressive Liberal Party (PLP), the first political party on the islands. Their stated goal was to prepare the majority population for eventual rule of the country.* To accomplish this objective, voter registration and education programs were started at the grassroots level. Literacy in the Bahamas had always been relatively high, but the populace, often being in remote areas, didn't exercise their right to vote. Their lack of participation in political affairs mirrored their lack of participation (and membership) in economic affairs as well.

Laborers had long been struggling for free

*To the British at that time, any mention of the Bahamas as a "country" as opposed to a "colony" was viewed as suspect.

trade unions at the workplace too. Wages and medical benefits were not their only concerns. Safety and guarantees against displacement were also high on the labor movement's agenda. Their exclusion from much of the building of Freeport was widely resented. Workers had protested against the government's willingness to grant exemptions from immigration laws permitting outside skilled and unskilled laborers to take high paying jobs that would otherwise go to island residents. The sense of resentment spilled over into other areas such as educational opportunities, social benefits and criminal justice procedures. In January 1958, the Bahamas Federation of Labour, representing the overwhelming majority of transportation and hospitality workers unions, declared a general strike. The federation was led by longtime trade unionist Randol Fawkes, a brave and energetic negotiator that management feared. It was under Fawkes' leadership that taxicab drivers struck in 1957 causing a three day shutdown of Nassau Airport. As February approached, and with it the peak tourist season, the strikes succeeded in debilitating all island commerce. When, after three weeks, the workers' demands were granted, thousands poured out into the streets of Nassau and elsewhere to celebrate.

The victory of labor and the passage of anti-discriminatory legislation by the assembly quickly broadened the appeal of the PLP. The next political challenge was voting rights. Up until that time, the colonial government had not permitted women or uneducated men to vote.

As primitive as this notion seems, universal suffrage was not allowed until 1961. In an attempt to diffuse the growing tide of anti-British sentiment, London passed a law in 1964 granting self-government to the Bahamas.

The convergence of these circumstances ensured a PLP majority in the general assembly in 1968, and by a resulting series of appointments, in the upper chamber too. Bahamian born, British educated attorney Lynden O. Pindling, as leader of the PLP, was now entitled to become the islands' executive officer. The British Parliament quickly responded by amending the Bahamas designation, dropping it as a colony and granting instead the status

The Great Seal of The Commonwealth of the Bahamas featuring the national motto.

"Commonwealth". This small but important change allowed Pindling to become the first Prime Minister of the Commonwealth of the Bahamas.

The question of full independence quickly arose. British and American interests advocated maintaining the status quo. The assembly, however, led by the PLP, voted in favor of independence by a large margin in 1972. On July 10, 1973, Prince Charles of England presented Prime Minister Pindling with the new Constitution of the Bahamas. It was a lavish, but symbolic ceremony which signified Great Britain's formal grant of independence. In a moment that shines on in the hearts of the Bahamian people, their new flag was raised over Fort Charlotte and the newly composed national anthem "March on Bahamaland" made its debut.* The Bahamas, while fully independent, chose to remain a member of the British Commonwealth, and so accordingly still recognizes Queen Elizabeth II as head of state. The Queen is represented by a Governor General. The Bahamas was accepted as a member of the United Nations on September 18, 1973.

The peaceful transition that the Bahamas enjoyed from island outpost to modern nation is certainly rare in world history. Instead of pro-

---

*The Bahamian flag is composed of a black triangle pointing into horizontal stripes, one gold stripe in the center, which is flanked by blue stripes on the top and bottom. The triangle represents the people; the gold stripe represents the land and the two blue stripes represent the sea.

tracted violence and revolution, the Bahamas checkered historical experience resulted instead in a slow growth of independence. The liberation of Asian and African colonies by the European powers in the 1950's and the U.S. civil rights movement undoubtedly hastened Bahamian independence. In 1979, the Bahamas celebrated its 250th anniversary of uninterrupted parliamentary democracy.

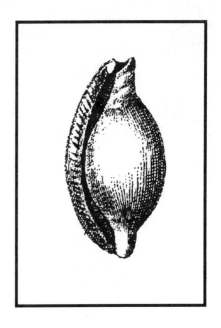

n the 1980's and 1990's, the Bahamas truly became an international tourist destination. Nearly four million visitors a year come to lay in the warm sun, swim in the ocean and enjoy the many tropical pleasures the islands have to offer. But tourism should not cloud the real story of life on the islands. All the development has not changed the solitude and singularity that still exists on the Family Islands, where the sprawling Atlantic meets the Caribbean. Here the island culture remains essentially unspoiled. Fishing, straw weaving and shipcrafting are all still practiced in the traditional, time-proven ways.

The Goombay Summer Festival held all over the islands each year from June through September is a popular extension of the islands cultural heritage. Goombay is a form of rhythmic beat music that has its roots in the mask dance rituals of East Africa. It is popular throughout the Caribbean, called "Gombey" in Bermuda and "Gombay" in Jamaica, but has survived in its primitive best on the Bahamas. During the festival, music and dancing celebra-

tions occur almost every night, as do street fairs, sporting events and water shows.

During the Christmas and New Year season, all Bahamians turn out for the annual Junkanoo parades, the island's answer to New Orleans' Mardi Gras. The Junkanoo tradition dates back at least two hundred years. It is really just a big fair, consisting of competing troupes of masqueraders who dance through the streets to the heavy beat of goatskin drums and rhythmic chants. The costumes they wear are made from colorful strips of crepe paper and dyed cloth. The Junkanoo Museum in Nassau provides visitors with a tour through the history of Junkanoo holidays and exhibits elaborate cos-

Sir Milo Butler, the first Governor General of the independent Bahamas

tumes from the past.

Over the past two decades, international banking and finance have found a home on the island of New Providence. A large influx of foreign banks were drawn to the Bahamas by a number of important factors including its political stability, secrecy laws, and the fact that the island also has no sales or inheritance taxes. Today, more than 350 financial institutions have branch offices in the Bahamas. The financial district in downtown Nassau has served as a solid economic counterbalance to tourism, which accounts for approximately two thirds of the country's annual gross national product.

The popularity of the Bahamas today contrasts markedly with the neglect of the islands in settler days. Beautiful year round weather, gambling casinos, fashionable beaches, big game fishing, sparkling waters, friendly bays and coral reefs hosting a myriad of lifeforms; all of these attractions and more make the Bahamas an ideal holiday paradise. Moreover, close proximity to Florida and the rise in popularity of cruise vacations has resulted in a level of prosperity not found elsewhere in the region. The Bahamas is at once, a new world Riviera and a sleepy, starry-eyed island nation. The major urban areas feature every modern convenience and excellent medical facilities. Main roads are smooth, making inter-island travel a popular pastime vacation adventure. With each progressively farther island from Nassau, the influence of tourism grows more faint and totally disappears in hundreds of small cays and secluded villages.

Many small islands are privately owned and so are off-limits to tourists. Transportation to countless locations in the out-islands is sometimes cumbersome, requiring air, sea and road travel in succession. Considering the size and shape of the area, it's not difficult to imagine that many quaint villages and fishing ports will remain quiet and remote for a long time to come. Though pockets of poverty still exist, the per capita income of the Bahamas is among the highest in the Americas. With a total population of only about 260,000, the Commonwealth of the Bahama Islands is destined to serve as a model of social and economic development for the entire Caribbean region.

Lynden O. Pindling, the first and long time Prime Minister of the Bahamas.

Commencement ceremonies at the College of The Bahamas in Nassau.

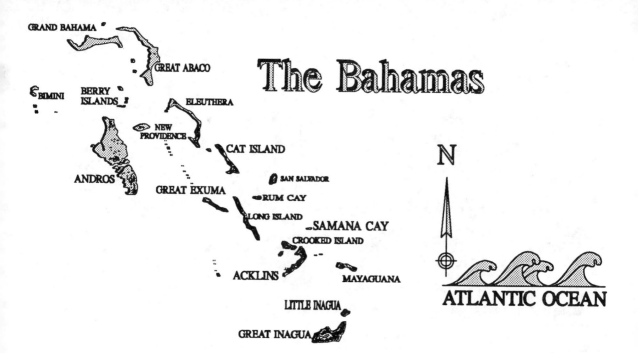

The Bahamas

GRAND BAHAMA

GREAT ABACO

BIMINI   BERRY ISLANDS

ELEUTHERA

NEW PROVIDENCE

CAT ISLAND

ANDROS

SAN SALVADOR

GREAT EXUMA

RUM CAY

LONG ISLAND   SAMANA CAY

CROOKED ISLAND

ACKLINS   MAYAGUANA

LITTLE INAGUA

GREAT INAGUA

N

ATLANTIC OCEAN

NEW PROVIDENCE AND PARADISE ISLAND

New Providence Island is the heart and brain of the Bahamas. Nassau, the country's capital city and major metropolitan area is located on its northeastern coast. Paradise Island hovers just offshore and spans out a mile or so to the east and west. Paradise Bridge connects the two islands in order to facilitate both vehicular and pedestrian traffic.

Nassau combines Old World charm with modern urban living. Tourists admire the colonial architecture of Parliament Square, the shopping on Bay Street and Nassau's many excellent restaurants. The island offers beautiful beaches, water sports, gardens, caves and wildlife preserves. Las Vegas style casino resorts are featured on newly developed Cable Beach, as well as on Paradise Island.

Nassau International Airport makes travel into and out of the islands very convenient. Inter-island flights are also available to all points in the out islands from the airport. Lake Kilarney in the center of the island is the major inland water resource for New Providence's 450,000 residents.

Some points of interest are the Nassau Botanical Gardens, the Straw Market in Market Plaza, Potter's Cay, Prince George Wharf (which features marvelous glass bottom boat rides), the Woode Rogers Nature Walk, Fort Charlotte, Fort Fincastle and the Water Tower, and of course, the Sea Gardens and French Cloisters of Paradise Island.

GRAND BAHAMA ISLAND

Grand Bahama is the second largest of the Bahamas islands spanning east and west almost eighty miles in total. Its western tip is the closest point between Florida and The Bahamas. The cosmopolitan center of Freeport/Lucaya is the major tourist destination. Crystal clear beaches, beautiful offshore coral reefs, two major casinos and renowned golf courses are just some of its major attractions. The International Bazaar in downtown Freeport is a quaint city-within-a-city featuring outdoor cafes, shops, restaurants and personal services. The nightlife on Grand Bahama is full of native Bahamian rhythms and glamorous song and dance venues.

The secluded West End of the island is the newest major resort district of the Bahamas. It can be reached by air (just 20 minutes from West Palm Beach, Florida) or by car via the scenic southern coastal highway which serves as the "spine" of the island. Grand Bahamas' interior and jagged north shore are mostly rocky and barren except for about two dozen small and scattered fishing villages that dot the ancient landscape.

Some particular attractions there are the

Rand Memorial Nature Centre, the beautiful Garden of the Groves, the Underwater Explorer's Museum and Grand Bahama Museum, where one can learn all about the Lucayan Indians, the islands' historical struggle and the Junkanoo holiday tradition.

A^{BACO}

Abaco is an outer cluster of islands and cays which span in a northwesterly manner half surrounding Grand Bahama Island to the west. Due to its many cays, bends and natural formations, it is a favorite cruising ground for yachtsman from all over the world. Marsh Harbor, Hope Town, Green Turtle Cay and Treasure Cay are just a few of the popular ports of call each featuring excellent maritime facilities. A candy-striped lighthouse in Hope Town was first built by the British more than 150 years ago. At Man-o-War Cay, shipbuilders still practice the techniques of their ancestors in the carving and shaping of traditional wooden boats. All of the major towns are connected by a main roadway which traverses the entire length of the long island, except for several ferry points, where bridges have not been erected. For serious divers, there is Pelican Cay National Park, on a beautiful coral and tropical fish preserve, where even night diving is permitted.

A^{NDROS}

The beauty and quiet of Andros, the largest island in the Bahamas, are two of its enchanting qualities, but its Great barrier reef is certainly the most magnificent. Stretching for more than 100 miles along the island's eastern coast, it is believed to be the second largest reef in the world. Amid its colorful coral garden depths remain remnants of old ship wrecks. The interior of Andros is still essentially untouched and remains the largest unexplored land area of all the islands.

Andros waters are also popular with big game fishermen. Known as the "Bone Fishing Capital of the World", popular catches are yellowtail, grunts, grouper, snapper, amberjack and angel fish. The islands deeper waters often yield swordfish, sturgeon, bluefin and many larger varieties. Despite the color and quiet of Andros, it is the home of AUTEC (Atlantic Underwater Testing and Evaluation Center) a joint British-U.S. facility which specializes in submarine communications research. According to island legend, Andros' forests are home to the "chickcharnies", magical, red-eyed elfish creatures who hang from trees and have a penchant for mischief.

BIMINI

Due to its proximity to Miami, Bimini has become popular sailing and fishing grounds. It's a small group of islands comprised of a southern island plain, which straddles a boomerang shaped cluster of islands and cays to its north.

Its warm inland waters and hot springs gave rise to the Juan Ponce de Leon's mystical Fountain of Youth. Alice Town on North Bimini island is the major visitor destination and largest town with a population of 40,000.

Bimini is famous for its big game fishing clubs. Record size marlin, wahoo tuna and sailfish have been plucked from the waters for years. American author Ernest Hemingway lived in Bimini's Blue Marlin Cottage from 1931-1937. It's a popular tourist attraction because of its display of Hemingway writings and memorabilia. Bimini is easily accessible via water or air from Miami, Nassau or Freeport.

ELEUTHERA, HARBOR ISLAND AND SPANISH WELLS

Eleuthera's pink sand beaches, secluded coves and dramatic rocky cliffs help make it a popular vacation destination for those who want to avoid the hustle of Nassau or the bustle of Freeport/Lucaya. Here is the islands first permanent colony of British settlers from the mid-1600's.

Eleuthera is a long and narrow island in the center of the Bahamian archipelago. It is never wider than a couple of miles from shore to shore. The gulf stream and warm sun help keep her waters warm and sparkling. The island is full of water sports facilities, from sailing to surfing and from water-skiing to skin diving. Intra-island travel, which was formerly by boat, is now made easy with the main north/south highway which stretches from Bannerman Town in the south to Gregory Town in the north, a distance of about 75 miles.

Harbor Island is a narrow stretch of land which juts out of the main island and consequently helps form a natural harbor at the top of Eleuthera. Spanish Wells Island lies beyond the harbor just offshore. Both places were popular holiday retreats for the rich and famous in the days before World War II. The stately homes and colonial style architecture of Dunmore Town on Harbor Island make it a quaint site for tourists to visit. Preachers Cave on Spanish Wells is also a popular tourist attraction because of the fateful history as the refuge of Sayle's adventurers in pre-colonial days.

EXUMA

The Exumas are a group of 365 islands which stretch out along a north-south crest about 50 miles long. The two largest islands are called Great Exuma and Little Exuma. The major town, George Town, is at the center of the main chain on the island's northern coast. Like on Eleuthera, one can sense the differences between the waters of the Atlantic and the Caribbean on many points on the islands of Exuma.

Snorklers and divers find Exuma National Land and Sea Park to be a real treat. Other past times for tourists are island hopping by boat, fishing, and in mid-April, The Family Island Regatta in Elizabeth Harbor. In North Exuma, at Steveton, lay the Loyalist Tombs, the final resting place of many British soldiers and explorers.

SAN SALVADOR

Originally called Guanahani by the Lucayan Indians, this beautiful island was renamed by Christopher Columbus on October 12, 1492, when he landed in the New World. San Salvador, which means Holy Saviour, is a quiet, peaceful island, much the same today as it was when Columbus first set foot on shore. Swim, fish, skin-dive or admire the beauty of its lush interior- much of it covered by fresh water lakes. One can visit one or all four of the sites where it is thought Columbus actually landed. And if you're there on Discovery Day (October 12), watch local "smack" boats race for glory and the winner's trophy at this fun-filled celebration.

San Salvador is unique among the Bahamas for its many inland lakes. Water makes up almost half of this islands 100 square miles. Cockburn Town on its central-west coast is its major town.

INAGUA

The third largest and most southerly of the Family Islands, Inagua is the home of one of the world's largest colonies of flamingos. Up to 40,000 live on Lake Windsor, 12 miles of shallow, marshy waters which form a wild lifepreserve to protect these beautiful pink-red birds. One can arrange a tour of the preserve by writing to The Bahamas National Trust, PO Box 4105, Nassau, New Providence, Bahamas; or call (809) 323-1317. Matthew Town, population 8,000, is the largest town on this sparsely populated island.

LONG ISLAND

One of the most scenic of the Family Islands, Long Island has 60 miles of powdery white beaches on the gentle sound and rocky, rugged headlands which descend suddenly to the ocean. Diving in the Long Island area is excellent. Trips to dive sites such as Conception Island, where one can explore over 30 shipwrecks, are conducted from Stella Maris, a complete resort complex at the northern end of the island. In May, the annual Long Island Regatta at Salt Pond, attracts many yachtsmen to this island, which is divided by the Tropic of Cancer.

BERRY ISLANDS

Quiet, beautiful and inviting, these 30 small islands lie 42 miles from Andros, close to the excellent fishing grounds on the banks and equally close to the challenge of deep water.

Divers can admire the underwater rock formations and 15-foot staghorn coral reefs off Mamma Rhoda Rock, or investigate an unidentified shipwreck with several cannon on board. The Stirrups Cay Lighthouse, built in 1863, on this delightful island is a favorite of cruise ships, which stop by so passengers can picnic and swim.

CAT ISLAND

Cat Island, named for British Sea Captain William Catt, will surprise you with its rolling hills and lush, green forests. Miles of deserted, windblown beaches, lend to some of the island's rich history and interesting sites. Explore the Arawak Indian caves near Port Howe, where you might uncover a pre-Columbian artifact. Visit the mansion and plantation built by Captain Andrew Deveaux, who recaptured Nassau from the Spanish in 1783. Don't miss the highest point in The Bahamas, at "Mount" Alvernia, all of 206 feet above sea level--but nonetheless impressive. Follow the Stations of the Cross carved along the winding path which leads to the spot where Father Jerome hand-built the Hermitage. And on the northern end of the island is Arthur's Town, boyhood home of actor Sidney Poitier. New Bright and Hawks Nest are the busiest towns on this golf club shaped island.

ACKLINS AND CROOKED ISLAND

For the remote and unhurried vacationer, a tranquil getaway in the Acklins or on Crooked Island may be ideal.

The hilly and serene Acklins can be reached by regularly scheduled Bahamain flights. Discover golden shores, dotted with scenic coves and hidden bays, with excellent bonefishing. For a bit of history, visit the quaint and charming old towns of Snug Corner, Lovely Bay, Delectable Bay or Pompey Bay, with its beautiful old church.

Just a short ride from the Acklins by ferry, lies Crooked Island. There one can explore its miles of deep creeks and tidal flats, filled with record tarpon and bonefish, which make Crooked Island a fisherman's delight. Stroll through charming villages as you pass citrus groves and breathe in the scent of the native herbs, which gave the island its reputation as one of "the fragrant islands."

This is not a complete description of the islands. With more than 700 islands to choose from, The Bahamas are simply too vast a chain to adequately describe in a book such as this. Among the other islands which play a role in the Bahamas story are Mayaguana, Little Inagua, Rum Cay and the Ragged Island Range.

Parliament Square in central Nassau celebrates both The Bahama's British legacy and the fact that the nation is North America's oldest democracy.

Photograph by John Penrod, used with permission.

FOR FURTHER READING

Albury, Paul   The Story of The Bahamas, MacMillan Caribbean, 1975

Bethel, A. T.   The Early Settlers of The Bahama Islands, Nassau, 1914

Craton, Michael   A History of The Bahamas, Collins, 1962

Dupuch, Eitenne, Jr.   Bahamas Handbook, Tribune Publishing, annual

Jane, C.   Editor The Journal of Christopher Columbus, Oxford Press, 1960

Peggs, A.D.   A Short History of The Bahamas, Nassau, 1960

Riggs, J. L.   Bahama Islands, New York, 1949

This is a short list of other sources. There are countless other interesting older works still available recounting the colonial period first hand. In addition, numerous travel guide books and boating manu are regularly published and updated which contain information helpful for tourists. The author strongly encourages their use.

ORDER FORM

QUANITY	TITLE	UNIT COST	TOTAL
	Hawaii : A Colorful and Concise History	$3.95	
	The Bahamas : A Colorful and Concise History	3.95	
	The Island of the Caribbean : A Colorful and Concise History	3.95	
	Mexico : A Colorful and Concise History	3.95	

Yes, please send me the books indicated above, Add $1.25 shipping and handling for the first book and $.50 for each additional book. Add $2.00 to total for books shipped to Canada or Hawaii. Overseas postage will be billed. Allow up to 4 weeks for delivery. Send check or money order payable to Scrivener Press. No cash or C.O.D.'s please. Quantity discounts available on request.

Subtotal	
Shipping & Handling	
MI residents add 4% sales tax	
TOTAL	

SEND BOOKS TO

NAME:_____

ADDRESS_____

CITY_____STATE____ZIP_____

Scrivener Press

P.O. Box 37175
Oak Park, MI 48237
(313) 546-9123 FAX (313) 546-3010
Phone orders by credit card : (800) 345-0096